HUNTING AND FISHING

A KID'S GUIDE

We're Going TURKEY HUNTING

Jonathan Potter

PowerKiDS press.

New York

Published in 2017 by The Rosen Publishing Group, Inc.
29 East 21st Street, New York, NY 10010

First Edition

Editor: Melissa Raé Shofner
Book Design: Tanya Dellaccio

Photo Credits: Cover david scott dodd/Shutterstock.com; back cover, pp. 1, 3–4, 6–8, 10, 12, 14–16, 18, 20–22, 24, 26, 28–32 ArtBitz/Shutterstock.com; all pages except p. 2 sittipong/Shutterstock.com; p. 5 Brandon Seidel/Shutterstock.com; p. 7 (wild turkey) Bruce MacQueen/Shutterstock.com; p. 7 (domestic turkey) V. Belov/Shutterstock.com; p. 9 James.Pintar/Shutterstock.com; p. 10 Troy Kellogg/Shutterstock.com; p. 11 Chris Turner/Shutterstock.com; p. 13 Dewayne Flowers/Shutterstock.com; p. 15 (hunter) studio0411/Shutterstock.com; p. 15 (shotgun) Scharfsinn/Shutterstock.com; pp. 17, 23, 30 Jordan Siemens/Getty Images; p. 19 Braxton Bruce Photography/Getty Images; p. 21(hunter)/ Bryan Eastham/Shutterstock.com; p. 21 (turkey tracks) Sharon Day/Shutterstock.com; p. 22 Jay Petersen/Shutterstock.com; pp. 24 (slate call), (gobbler call), 25, 27 Jeffrey B. Banke/Shutterstock.com; p. 24 (box call) Stephanie Frey/Shutterstock.com; p. 29 (turkey chick) almondd/Shutterstock.com; p. 29 (turkey family) https://commons.wikimedia.org/wiki/File:Wild_turkey_with_chicks.jpg.

Cataloging-in-Publication Data
Names: Potter, Jonathan.
Title: We're going turkey hunting / Jonathan Potter.
Description: New York : PowerKids Press, 2017. | Series: Hunting and fishing: a kid's guide| Includes index.
Identifiers: ISBN 9781499427462 (pbk.) | ISBN 9781499428698 (library bound) | ISBN 9781508152842 (6 pack)
Subjects: LCSH: Turkey hunting–Juvenile literature.
Classification: LCC SK325.T8 P68 2017 | DDC 799.2'4645–dc23

Manufactured in the United States of America

CPSIA Compliance Information: Batch Batch #BW17PK: For Further Information contact Rosen Publishing, New York, New York at 1-800-237-9932

CONTENTS

A NOTE TO READERS

Always talk with a parent or teacher before proceeding with any of the activities found in this book. Some activities require adult supervision.

A NOTE TO PARENTS AND TEACHERS

This book was written to be informative and entertaining. Some of the activities in this book require adult supervision. Please talk with your child or student before allowing them to proceed with any hunting activities. The author and publisher specifically disclaim any liability for injury or damages that may result from use of information in this book.

HISTORY OF THE HUNT

Wild turkeys are originally from North America. Hunting these large birds has been an important and popular activity for a long time. Native Americans have hunted them for thousands of years. Turkeys are even **sacred** to some native peoples. Native Americans often wear turkey feathers in their headdresses. European settlers saw turkeys for the first time when they arrived in the New World.

Today, turkeys are still important in the United States. Millions of Americans eat turkey for Thanksgiving dinner each year.

HUNTING HINT

Wild turkeys are big birds. Males can weigh more than 20 pounds (9 kg).

Benjamin Franklin once suggested that the turkey would make a better national bird for the United States than the bald eagle.

TASTY TURKEYS

Turkey makes a tasty meal and not just on Thanksgiving. People eat turkey all year round. Most of the turkey we eat comes from farms. These birds have been fattened up, most often on corn. Wild turkeys don't taste quite like **domestic** ones.

Many turkey hunters prefer the meat of wild turkeys to the turkey meat sold in stores. They also enjoy the **challenge** presented by these birds in the wild. Working hard to hunt a turkey makes the meat taste even better.

HUNTING HINT

In the wild, turkeys are **omnivores**. They eat plants and also hunt for insects and other small creatures.

Unlike turkeys in the wild, domestic turkeys raised on farms are often white.

HUNTING SEASON

Like many animals, turkeys are in season during the fall and sometimes the winter. A season is the time when you're allowed to hunt a certain animal. Most states also have spring gobbler seasons. Gobblers, or toms, are male turkeys. They're much larger and provide more meat than females, which are called hens.

Some hunters consider fall turkey hunting to be better sport because it's more challenging. It's harder to get gobblers to come to you in the autumn. Turkey hunting is allowed in most states between sunup and sundown.

HUNTING HINT

Turkey-hunting rules are different from state to state. Be sure to check your state's laws online before going hunting.

Hens can be hunted in the fall in some states. Check your state's rules and don't shoot hens if they're out of season.

INTO THE FOREST

In the wild, turkeys live in forested areas and grassy fields. They avoid thick brush, or plants that grow close to the ground. Successful turkey hunters pick spots in the woods that offer clear views for shooting.

Turkey hunting is permitted on state game lands. These are large natural areas owned by the government. Wild turkeys can also be hunted on private property if the owner allows it. Always ask before hunting on someone's land. Never hunt on land where "No Hunting" signs are posted.

Wild turkeys must find their own food. They're far more active than turkeys raised on farms. This gives their meat a stronger taste.

HUNTING HINT

Before you go turkey hunting, know your state's bag limit. This is the total number of turkeys you're allowed to shoot each season.

WHAT TO WEAR

Many hunters wear orange for safety. However, turkeys can see colors. Therefore, hunters wear **camouflage** when turkey hunting. Camouflage patterns help hunters blend in with the woods. It's a good idea to wear camouflage gloves to hide the color of your hands and a camouflage mask or makeup to hide your face.

Turkey feathers can be red, white, blue, brown, or black. It's not a good idea to wear these colors while hunting. Another hunter might mistake you for a gobbler in the forest.

HUNTING HINT

Wild turkeys can run up to 25 miles (40.2 km) per hour. They can also fly for short **distances** at speeds up to 55 miles (88.5 km) per hour.

The pattern on this hunter's clothing makes him harder to see. Some states require turkey hunters to wear a bit of bright orange, so make sure you know the rules for your area.

THE RIGHT GUN

A shotgun is the best firearm, or gun, for turkey hunting. Shotguns shoot shells that are tightly packed with small pellets called shot. The shot explodes out of the gun and scatters in a small area.

Shotguns have a shorter range than rifles do. In order to get a good shot, a hunter must get close to a turkey. Killing a gobbler from more than 40 yards (37 m) away isn't easy and doesn't happen often. Clean and oil your gun when the season ends.

HUNTING HINT

Never point a gun at yourself or another person. Always keep your shotgun's safety on until you're ready to fire.

A turkey hunter loads, or puts a shell into, a shotgun. Different kinds of shotguns are loaded in different ways.

PRACTICE YOUR SHOT

It's harder to shoot a shotgun than you might think. It takes a lot of practice to learn to aim and shoot well. Sporting clubs often have shooting ranges where hunters can use their firearms. You should practice at a shooting range long before you hit the woods.

Practice will help you shoot in tight patterns. In other words, you'll be more likely to hit your **target**. **Estimating** distances will also become easier after shooting at a range.

HUNTING HINT

Never fire your gun until you're absolutely sure of your target.

Like other hunters, turkey hunters must prove they know how to safely use a gun before they can get a hunting **license**.

USING A BOW

For a greater challenge, you can hunt turkeys with a bow. Modern compound bows are more advanced than the ones used in the past. Compound bows use cables and **pulleys** that make it easier to pull back an arrow.

It's important to purchase the correct arrowheads. Broadheads are the best for turkey hunting. These arrowheads are triangular and have sharp edges. Bowhunters must have excellent aim in order to hit their target. It's a good idea to practice using a bow before heading off on a hunt.

HUNTING HINT

Whether you hunt with a bow or a shotgun, you'll need to take a safety course and get your hunting license. Visit your state's wildlife department website to learn more.

This turkey hunter is using a compound bow.

GETTING TO KNOW THE LAND

If you can, explore the area in which you hope to hunt before turkey season begins. You can learn to follow tracks, and you might even see some turkeys. You can discover where they travel and find the best spots for shooting them. Getting to know the area will also prevent you from getting lost.

It's important to pick a good hunting spot. Sitting with your back against a large object is a good idea, so look for a place with big rocks and trees.

HUNTING HINT

Try to get a map of the area if you plan to hunt on public lands.

Having something wide behind you, such as a big tree, makes it harder for a turkey to see the shape of your body.

turkey tracks

ON THE HUNT

Hunters must get gobblers to come to them. This makes hunting turkey different from hunting other kinds of animals. For example, some animals are best hunted by stalking them. When you stalk an animal, it means you follow it closely and secretly. This is a very bad idea when hunting gobblers. It's almost impossible to sneak up on one. It's also unsafe. Remember, turkey hunters don't usually wear orange. What you think is a turkey might actually be another turkey hunter!

Sometimes turkey hunters use a blind. A blind is a screen that hides a hunter from their prey.

HUNTING HINT

You should learn about the places where gobblers can be found. This will help you pick a good hunting spot.

DECOYS AND CALLS

Some turkey hunters use decoys, which are fake animals. Calls are tools used to imitate, or copy, the sounds made by turkeys. Decoys and calls can trick real turkeys into coming closer to you.

Be careful, though. Decoys and calls can also fool hunters. Always cover a decoy with camouflage when you carry it. You don't want another hunter shooting at a decoy while it's in your hands. If you think another hunter is nearby, you shouldn't make turkey calls.

slate call

gobbler call

box call

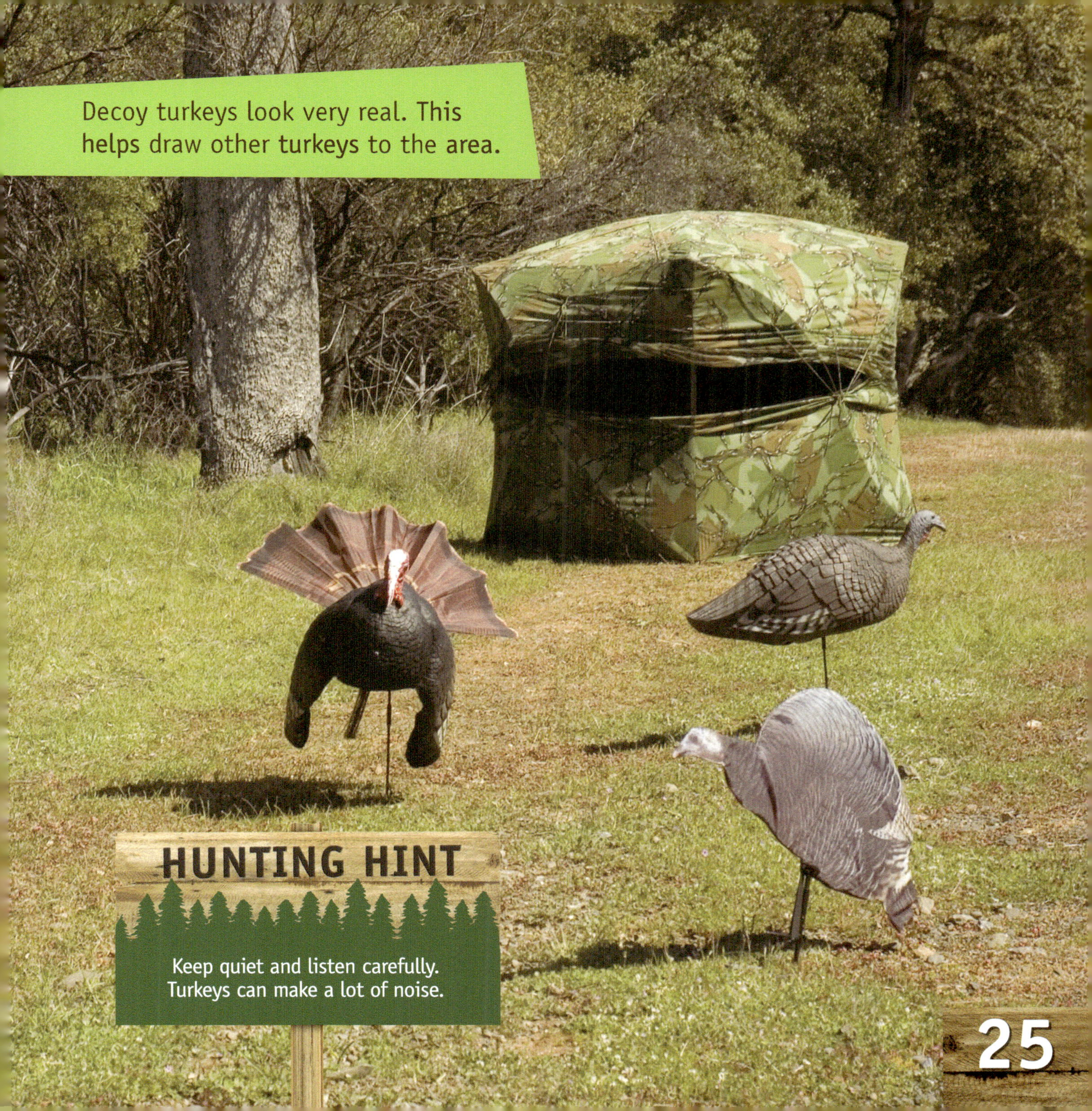

Decoy turkeys look very real. This helps draw other turkeys to the area.

HUNTING HINT

Keep quiet and listen carefully. Turkeys can make a lot of noise.

ENJOYING YOUR TURKEY

If you shoot a turkey, the first thing you must do is field dress it. Field dressing, or cleaning, your kill prevents the meat from going bad. It's always smart to bring a sharp knife, garbage bags, and plastic gloves on your hunt. You don't have to remove the feathers until you get the bird home. You must also fill out the tag from your hunting license and tag your bird. This helps your state keep track of turkey populations.

HUNTING HINT

Your wild turkey won't taste exactly like a **traditional** Thanksgiving dinner. Remember that wild turkeys taste different from domestic ones.

This hunter was lucky enough to shoot two turkeys. These large **birds** are heavy, so make sure you have a plan for getting yours home!

SAVING WILD TURKEYS

Just 70 years ago, there were only 30,000 wild turkeys left in North America. They nearly died out because people were overhunting them and destroying their forest **habitats**. We're lucky that wild turkeys are still around today.

Groups such as the National Wild Turkey Federation (NWTF) have worked hard to bring the turkey back. Hundreds of hunters have joined the NWTF to help save wild turkey habitats. Thanks to groups like the NWTF, North America has millions of wild turkeys once again.

Efforts to grow wild turkey populations have been very successful. Today, wild turkeys are found in every U.S. state except Alaska.

HUNTING HINT

Wild turkey chicks are able to follow their mothers around and find food very soon after they break out of their shells.

RESPECT FOR THE SPORT

While it's true that hunters kill wild animals for sport, it's important to remember that good hunters have respect for nature. Hunters enjoy the natural world, and they fight to keep it safe. Thanks to them, wild turkeys have made a huge comeback.

Turkey hunting has been important in North America for many years. The skills of hunting are often handed down from parent to child. Hunters are proud of these traditions. Turkey hunting will continue to be a popular activity for many years to come.

GLOSSARY

camouflage: A clothing pattern that soldiers and hunters wear to make them harder to see.

challenge: Something requiring extra effort.

distance: The space between two points.

domestic: Bred and raised for use by people.

estimate: To make a careful guess about an answer based on the known facts.

habitat: The natural home for plants, animals, and other living things.

license: An official paper giving someone the right to do something.

omnivore: An animal that eats both plants and animals.

pulley: A wheel or set of wheels used with a rope or chain to lift or lower heavy objects.

sacred: Highly respected and considered very important.

target: Something that is aimed at.

tradition: Something in a culture that is passed down from parents to children.

INDEX

WEBSITES

Due to the changing nature of Internet links, PowerKids Press has developed an online list of websites related to the subject of this book. This site is updated regularly. Please use this link to access the list: www.powerkidslinks.com/hunt/trky